Creative Visualization Techniques

Visualize a Successful Future

Hattie Spiritweaver

ISBN: 9781514184523

DISCLAIMER

CONTENTS

ACKNOWLEDGMENTS

There are many people to thank on this awesome journey called life. I've had many great mentors and met various people along the way who contributed to my path of success.

Each one of them played a role and part in encouraging me to become my best authentic self. I appreciate every one of you, and there are too many to account around the globe. You all know who you are, and whether it was big or small I am grateful for each and every one of you. Now it's time to pay it forward

1 CHAPTER
WHAT IS CREATIVE VISUALIZATION

Whether we know it or not, our imagination creates scenario's and stories every day. We see with our physical eyes. We see buildings, flashing signs, people walking by, cars flying down the highway and we interact with what we see.

We can see an image on the television or computer screen. We can see an image of any photograph.

Whenever we look at a photograph, what's happening in front of us, or watch and image on a screen we are drawn into the image, and our minds start creating a story.

We may see a small girl riding her bicycle, and assume, or conclude she is happy by the smile on her face, her body language, and the environment.

We do the same every day when we watch other people. We may not have any information about them, but make an observation, and assume and conclude what we perceive is happening in their lives.

We may fill in the blanks, and say, "She must be a

happy girl, well taken care of, and lives in a nice neighborhood. She's dressed in nice clothes, so her parents must be wealthy and rich."

This photograph can be deceptive. Perhaps, her grandmother bought the outfit, took the snapshot in her neighborhood, and the girl is poor and lives in a lower class environment.

In the film industry, we make observations. Even if we took all the audio out of a movie, we'd draw our own conclusions, assume what the story was about, and form a fictional story with our imagination.

If you place the audio back in the movie after it is over, and watch it from the beginning, we'd find out we have a completely different story, and it doesn't match with the original story.

If you were blind, you wouldn't see any color, or images. You would see with your hands, observe with your hands, and feel the shape and texture. You would smell, hear, and taste things.

Blind people can't see symbols. We create a shape, texture, or image and create a symbol. We give it a meaning, and say, this is what this means. The same for a blind person, they have to feel the object, texture, and give it a meaning.

When you're deaf, you can see, smell, taste, and feel the object. Again you don't know the story, or the meaning of the symbol, unless someone uses sign language, and tells you what it means.

A deaf person's imagination will try to take over and make sense out of what the person is observing, and take the information given, conclude and specify what is happening in their experience.

You will learn this, if you learn a new language or visit another country. We may not know what the symbols represent, or what the words mean until we learn from a native what it means and stands for in their particular country.

A symbol then only means what meaning you apply to the image, and what you believe it stands for by what others have told you in society or your particular culture.

Visualization is something we do every day whether we're aware of it or not. We also use our imagination, or the right side of our mind. The right side of the brain is where we draw conclusions, assume, and use our imagination to create our everyday reality.

Throughout the centuries since time began, artists have used their imagination by creating different masterpieces of art and literature.

What is reality? We say, "You should face reality." We all have our unique reality, experience, and perception. We observe and see things differently.

If we all witnessed the same events, we'd each have a different take on what happened in the experience.

We may agree with others, and think we're wrong, or we can be right, and go along with the crowd, because we want to fit in, be approved of, and we don't like being rejected. We will agree simply because we don't want to rock the boat, or cause conflict.

In the Asch Conformity Experiment, they showed people the same picture and asked what lines are longer or shorter. In the experiment the participants went along with the group, and thought they were wrong, or believed they were right, but went along with the group anyway.

We may doubt our perception and experience, but another person may disagree with us.

When we hear certain sounds without a visual, we again use our imagination. When we hear the sound of a train, we hear the wheels on the track, and we hear the whistle, this will trigger our memory and give us a mental image of a train.

We can say the same thing happens when we read a book with no visual. We see the words, know a meaning, and visualize what the person looks like, what they may act like, and sound like. Certain key words trigger our five senses, sight, hearing, smelling, tasting, and feeling.

When we're in an argument, a mental image of the past is triggered by the vocabulary someone speaks.

We relate the current experience with the past, and we draw a conclusion, or assume the same experience will occur again. We project the old reality on the person who is standing in front of us now.

We get in a negative mindset, carry negative thoughts, and have a negative attitude. We visualize those old experiences and project them on to the present and the future. We believe again, what we've experienced in the past will reflect on this present moment. We struggle with change, because we keep our focus on the past results, instead of trying new things.

Creative Visualization is when we create in our mind a certain mental image and project it on to the present experience. What is the idea of visualization? It is to bring clarity, clear concise mental images of how you would like to see your life and future.

Not everyone is a visual learner, and some people are naturally visual. We make a mistake in not acknowledging, visualization doesn't come naturally to everyone.

Visualization may or may not work for you, and like I already stated before, blind people, cannot visualize when they've never seen an image or symbol.

There are different types of learning styles.
Visual
Musical/Auditory
Verbal
Physical/Kinesthetic
Logical/Math
Social
Solitary

It's important to know what learning style you have and whether Visualization alone will help you.

Creative is using the imagination. They are two different things, and maybe why people learn from stories, and parables.

You cannot succeed at visualization if you simply can't visualize. Visualization may not be the answer for you.

2 CHAPTER
CLARITY

For us to succeed at visualization we would have to form a mental image of the thing, or circumstances we desire in life.

For example: If I wanted to graduate from college, or university, I would try to picture in my mind what this would look like?

This is where the vision board might be helpful. I would put up a picture of the University I would like to attend.

I know from this photograph what it looks like.

What does it smell like? I smell bake goods from the culinary arts class. I smell fresh made fries in the cafeteria. The fries taste salty, doused in tangy mustard, and crispy.

I see cars parked in a huge parking lot, I see security guards, and I see professors at the desk. I see a library filled with books and nice computers.

I feel positive and successful, because I have positive, and supportive professors who want me to achieve my dreams. I hear the lectures, and I hear music booming from the IPod during breaks.

While I have a vision board, and others believe this helps them, it doesn't help me as much as visualizing the experience during meditation, or watching motivational videos.

It may just be I'm a visual person and the vision board doesn't lead to action for me. It's stagnate, not moving, and doesn't encourage me to take action.

I have a vision board on my desktop, but it amounts to materialism, dreaming, wanting, and doesn't focus on action or movement.

After a while I get used to it being there, and don't even pay attention to it much. Like anything else, in our house, how many times do you notice everything in its place? You just get used to it being there.

By visualizing you're forcing yourself to participate in creating the experience during meditation. And not necessarily just in meditation. I can visualize any time anywhere, and with my eyes open.

Vision boards are good reminders of where we

want to be, and if you happen to pay attention to a vision board, and it helps you, this is good for you. Everyone learns differently.

Be precise and clear about what it is you want out of life.

Some people write a list in their journal or make a bucket list. Whatever works for you?

3 CHAPTER
WE CREATE OUR LIVES

From the time we were born until this very point in time, we've created our lives. We create every day, and visualize what kind of life we live.

If I ask you, "What do you look for in a husband or wife?" You will say something like, "I want someone with brown hair, six feet tall, mustache, no beard, he dresses like a businessman, and he talks like a cowboy."

Now look at your partner? He doesn't match up with your list.

When you picked out the last five men in your life, Joe, Harry, James, Nick, and Matteo, didn't wear a business suit, may or may not have had brown hair, and their height was different.

They might have shaved or had a mustache and beard. They wore suits to social functions, but weren't business men. And none of them talked like a cowboy. Instead you picked people based on what you learned growing up.

Let's say you have a negative mindset, belief system, and thought process. You were brought up by a business woman, but she was married to a drug addict who wasted all her money on drugs. They were divorced. Argued all the time, and one was very disciplined, strict, and harsh, while the other was lazy, disorganized, and didn't care about anything.

You then started dating, and the generational thinking patterns, habits, and behaviors came with you, from picking up their mindset, beliefs, and thoughts.

You have been the responsible one in all your past relationships, but the partners you choose reflect you father who was a drug addict.

You formed a habit of dating similar men who have some kind of addiction.

When you visualize, you have to be clear about what kind of relationship you want to have more than just the physical description.

"I want to have a healthy relationship?" What is healthy to you? Be clear about what healthy is?

For example:

"I want a relationship with a man who is

responsible with his mental health, emotional health, spiritual health, and physical health."

When you visualize what does a healthy man look like in action? He looks like a business man. He is dressed in a suit, he's on the cellphone talking to business professionals, he owns his own business, and he travels, and is organized.

"He's working out at the gym, he's bringing home flowers weekly, he's taking me out to dinner or events on the weekends, and he is attentive to my feelings, emotions, and thoughts."

"He listens to me and doesn't interrupt. He is tender and gentle with me physically. He doesn't harm me emotionally, mentally, physically, or spiritually. He kisses me, has sex with me in an appropriate manner, and cherishes our relationship."

"We get along. We can speak in a calm manner and not hide our feelings and thoughts. We don't take things personally or attack each other. We can listen to each other and respect each other."

"He smells like nice aftershave and cologne."
"He sounds good, his voice is soothing and calming to my soul."

"He tastes like chocolate, because he's always buying me a box of the best chocolate. He tastes like strawberries when we kiss."

As you can see you have to think clearly about what kind of man you want, and maybe even put up a picture of the type of man, or write in a journal to remind yourself every time you meet a man.

Does he fit the description or are you just settling. Are you being impatient, and not willing to wait for this guy to show up?

It's important to have a good idea of what you're creating in life. You can do this exercise with your friends as well.

What kind of people do you want to hang around? What kind of influence do they have on your life? And how does it have a cause and effect on your life.

What kind of career do you want to explore? Is it just a job at McDonald's, at a corporation, running your own business? Be direct about it.

What kind of House do you want to live in? What kind of car do you want to drive? Where do you want to travel?

4 CHAPTER
TAKING ACTION

What kind of action steps are you taking? What most people do is make a vision board and dream about it. They're thinking how wonderful it would be to get there, and not doing anything to get there.

What steps do you need to take to get there? Visualize yourself taking those steps and creating the future you desire.

In my own life, I use visualize in meditation. I also watch video's for the simple reason there is movement.

In the video someone is taking action steps to achieve their dreams. They're practicing, practicing, and practicing for hours and hours until they're the best. They're training every day.

They're mentally rehearsing every step. Sports athletes are very good at this, mentally rehearsing and using mental imagery to see themselves performing.

They're constantly training for hours and hours until they get their spirit, mind, and body in alignment to perform certain actions.

What is the point of the videos? The point is to remind you nothing happens in life without being clear, decisive, determined, and motivated, and driven to reach your goals. Everything action must be taken on purpose in the right direction.

We can visualize all day, but if we aren't mentally rehearsing the actions, and then taking them, we can't succeed.

We find ourselves stuck and unmotivated to take action because we allow negative thinking patterns and mindset sabotage our success. We must be focused on the goal. Turn off the noise from the audience. (Friends, family, strangers, and everyone else).

You have to see where you're going, and take one step at a time to get there. With negative thinking, and negative habits, we get negative results.

How does visualization work in a negative way? If you're visualizing everyday you're going to have divorce, a broken home, lack of finances, believe it's a dangerous world, and you're going to fail. If you believe this, it will happen.

You're focusing all your attention on the

negatives of the world creating it in your reality every day.

There are a million small steps to take to become a successful professional, have a healthy love relationship, and be successfully financially? What steps are you taking to get there?

If you're just staring at a vision board every day, you're not doing anything to get there. You're just dreaming, you're not making it happen.

If you're not training every day in personal development, spiritual development, in business, educating yourself for a certain profession, and a healthy love relationship you're not going to get there.

You have to want to succeed, not sit around and wait for life to happen. It will never happen. If you're waiting for someone else to motivate you and come along for the ride, you'll be waiting forever.

You're dreams belong to you. Your dreams don't matter to anyone else.

Visualize yourself taking actions every day. See yourself signing up for courses. See yourself studying. See yourself writing. See yourself reading. See yourself spending money wisely. See yourself doing every action step along the way.

Hear yourself saying Affirmations:

"I can do this."
"I can get past these fears."
"I am smart enough."
"I am emotionally strong enough."
"I am mentally tough."
"I have the patience and endurance to make it to my goal."
"I can get through every obstacle."
"It doesn't matter what people think or say."
"I can do whatever I believe I can do and imagine."

If affirmations don't work for you, listen to motivational videos.

Negative thoughts mixed with chaos and confusion distract us and delay us from moving forward in life.

Let go of the past.

5 CHAPTER
LET GO

We can be so stuck in the past failures, mistakes, and trauma and tragedy. Visualize letting go.

Visualize yourself sitting in a body of water. Feel the warmth of the lake. Feel the heat of the sun. Feel the soothing water rolling towards you and taking away the fears, anger, hurt, pain, and suffering. Watch them roll away back out to sea like drift wood which goes further and further away until you can't see it anymore.

Feel the water clearing away all the debris and releasing you from any negative feeling, emotion, or experience.

There are many visualizations and meditations to guide you through depression, anxiety, stress, fears, and other emotions, and feelings.

Visualization can help you see yourself whole and healthy.

How do you see yourself?

See yourself handling your emotions and feelings perfectly. See yourself handling naysayers, fault finders, and other negative parties in a neutral way. See yourself staying calm and unaffected by others.

Hear yourself speaking clearly, straight forward, and open and honest with yourself and others.

Visualize yourself smelling like your favorite perfume, bath gel, bubble bath, or favorite scent.

Visualize yourself tasting your favorite meals and snacks. Tasting healthy foods that are delicious and healthy.

Visualize yourself taking walks outside, running on the track, riding a bike, swimming, or hiking.

Visualize yourself feeling great, happy, and whole and complete.

Visualize yourself letting go of things which no longer work in your life. What's not working? The negative mindset, beliefs, thinking patterns, and habits. What needs to change?

6 CHAPTER
EXPECTATIONS

When we visualize we may have a certain idea what we want, but never think about if we will we do if we get what we want?

For example: If you visualize being successful at a career and money, do you know how to handle finances, invest, and make financial decisions?

What if you don't know, and this moment arrives where you have money? What will you do with it?

We have the expectations of, "If I have money, I can buy anything with it, I can go anywhere, and do anything my heart desires."

I don't believe there's anything wrong with this dreaming. On the other hand, if you spend all the money on luxury and dreams, and never invest it and allow your money to grow, you may be right back where you started after you had fun.

Many people who win the lottery, have a joy ride until their money runs out, but then they're flat broke, because they weren't responsible with the money.

Many famous people have done the same thing, and it is wise to study about successful people's lives and understand there is two sides of having success. It's all about your choices, and how you handle things.

If you're expecting to be successful, have loads of fun, and no worries, these are false expectations. There is responsibility in relationships, success, and finances.

7 CHAPTER
THE SUBCONSCIOUS & CONSCIOUS MIND

We really have to be mindful and self-aware. When we walk around the world with negative self-talk and listening to other people's fault finding and negative messages we take in all the negatives.

We take in negative information on a daily basis. We read negative content, watch negative content, and listen to negative content. It's our choice.

We really have to pay attention to whether we're filling our thoughts with positive or negative information. Our Subconscious really remembers everything we experience and what goes in must come out.

If we're filling it with negative things, we're going to regurgitate negative things. We're going to feel negative, be angry, hateful, disappointed, unloved, alone, depressed, and filled with anxiety.

When we use affirmations, devotions, prayers, positive quotes, or other healthy content, we can become wiser, calmer, more focused, think with clarity, and see things from a different angle and perspective.

We are self-conscious and worried about what other people think. We are conscious of what is happening around us if we're focused and paying attention.

When we're mindful and self-aware we can see the problem, but see what is wrong in the picture. We can see what needs to be adjusted in our own habits and thinking. We can observe and evaluate what is our issue, and what is someone else's.

We become aware, our thinking, becomes action, and becomes words. Those negative thoughts become weapons and have a cause and effect on the relationship between being successful in relationships and career or failing.

Words become our destruction besides our actions. Visualization helps us be aware of what kind of person we want to be, and seeing ourselves taking the right steps, by choosing wisely what kind of negative content we read or watch. It also helps us see ourselves hanging out with healthy mindsets who don't naysay, fault find, and abuse us.

Whatever we believe, think, and feel matters. If we're all tight, filled with anxiety, depression, and anger, we naturally react, and abuse others. If we feel yucky about ourselves and other people, they feel it too.

If we feel good about ourselves they feel good. And they can tell, by the way you talk to them, present yourself to them, and how you react rather than respond in a positive manner.

Clear out the junk you have stored up in your thoughts. Write it out in a journal, blog, paint, sculpt, draw, play sports, build sand castles, do something to dump all the negatives.

Unlearn negative thought patterns, behaviors, and habits. Learn positive ones and healthy ones. Visualize yourself succeeding and don't give up on yourself. Be patient. Have healthy expectations and don't compare yourself with other people. We're all at different stages of the game.

8 CHAPTER
EMOTIONS

Emotions and feelings really do have to come in alignment. If you're around negative people, and you're anxious, stressed, and in poor circumstances it shows up when you're interacting with others.

Try to remember and visualize times in your life when you won a trophy, graduated, a safe place, a safe person, and how it made you feel. Reflect on the events.

How did it make you feel? What were they saying? What were they doing? Why did you feel so excited, happy, and alive? What's it feel like to be unconditionally loved? Visualize those times, and remember all the actions you took. Remember the emotions, the feeling, and the ambience. What made it so special?

When you're having a bad day, you can shift your mood by listening to uplifting positive music. If you listen to different genre's you will notice different music and lyrics will make you feel differently. It will rise and fall depending on what you're listening too.

When you're creating something, you are feeling

peaceful, quiet, and calm. When you're involved in a creative activity, your imagination is creating an object, a piece of art work, a flower garden, a sculpture, a piece of music, or even a piece of furniture.

You're learning to use both your logical side and creative side and become more centered, by expanding your thinking.

At the same time your emotions are being released, anxiety, and stress. If you're not releasing the pressure, keeping everything inside, and dwelling on things, you're allowing yourself to be like a pressure cooker ready to explode. You usually are when you react or get snappy with someone.

Find a positive way to handle your emotions.

9 CHAPTER
VISION & STORY BOARDS

Vision/Story Boards can be very creative and fun. If vision boards help you, it's a great idea to remember what kind of life you desire. You can make a vision board with power point, and insert photographs from images online, and send it to your desktop.

Create a story with the pictures. What steps would it take to get to your biggest goal? Put them in order. You may put a picture of a successful women in a business suit first.

You're ready for success, nicely dressed to go to training.

This would be a photograph of a College/University, Trade School, Success Workshop, Relationships weekend retreat, diet center, or fitness center. This maybe pictures of reading, working out, running, studying, or working.

After you've learned the skills, you would pick images of you in that business setting, office, on the beach, in a certain country, state, or society.

How far do you want to go? You have lots of clients, lots of customers, and your products are a big success. There are great reviews and rewards.

You now have the images of traveling to different destinations. Meeting new people. Having new adventures, having fun, relaxing, and happy.

Everyone's story board will be different. There is no right or wrong way to create a story board.

You can make one on a poster board, frame it, and go to the arts and crafts store and find different feathers, beads, sequence, and use stencils. The art world is endless with supplies and ideas.

Visualization is something you already do every day. When you get up in the morning you see yourself having breakfast, getting the mail, driving out of the parking lot, and rolling in the office.

You see yourself heading to the bakery. When you think of that nice juicy steak, you picture it, taste it, feel the joy of it, and smell it. You usually ride over to your favorite steak house for lunch.

We really never think about it, but we do visualize every day. It's not as hard as we think it is, and it's really just being aware of what we're focusing on, and what we want to create.

10 CHAPTER
TIMING

Visualization doesn't happen overnight. It's not a quick fix. Life changes gradually over time.

This is why I say visualize by taking small steps, one day at a time. Never force yourself to achieve things. Allow yourself to relax.

Visualize yourself getting into an appropriate school, job, or relationship. Visualize training, practicing, and applying what you learn to your life in every situation.

I used to practice personal development skills on everyone I met every day online and offline. It doesn't matter where you are, the opportunity arrives.

When what you visualized comes true, you're sitting in the class room, on the job, or in the relationship. Still there is more visualizing to do.

Studying, learning, applying, and the more actions you take, the more rewards. If you show up for your job, you may move up the ladder, and you may get another job offer. Your relationship might turn better and better the more you change your attitude, thinking, and mindset.

There is always small steps, along the way. Everything happens when you're prepared and ready for it.

If you're not taking steps and actions, the opportunity will come and you won't be ready.

Timing is everything. The journey of life is a process, and even if you visualize, it doesn't mean things will happen in a flash. You still have to take the steps to improve yourself, and take the appropriate steps.

The process will take as long as you desire to take your time. If time is used wisely, and you take advantage of spare time, it's only a matter of time, before changes start happening. If you're always moving forward, visualizing and creating, time flies by before you know it.

Visualization & meditation both take time to learn. Some may learn it fairly quickly and other people may take 6 months up to a year before they are comfortable and disciplined. Many people become impatient, give up and quit because they aren't patient with themselves.

For any good habit to form, you have to do it whether you feel like it or not, and consistently every day.

Everything is hard when you first start doing it, and it gets easier the more you learn and move through it day by day.

Be patient with yourself. Take it one step at a time.

The resources in the now are available. The more you train and practice, the opportunities expand, more people notice, and there are more resources available.

If you play small, you get small results. If you play big, you will get plenty of opportunity. The more opportunities, the more successful you'll become.

HATTIE SPIRITWEAVER